I0616255

THE VOICE
of the SWORD

The Devil's Advocate

JOSEPH L. SINKFIELD

Copyright © 2025 by Joseph L. Sinkfield

ISBN: 979-8-88615-312-5 (Paperback)
       979-8-88615-313-2 (Hardback)
       979-8-88615-314-9 (Ebook)

All rights reserved. No part of this publication may be reproduced, distributed, or transmitted in any form or by any means, including photocopying, recording, or other electronic or mechanical methods, without the prior written permission of the publisher, except in the case brief quotations embodied in critical reviews and other noncommercial uses permitted by copyright law.

The views expressed in this book are solely those of the author and do not necessarily reflect the views of the publisher, and the publisher hereby disclaims any responsibility for them.

Inks and Bindings
888-290-5218
www.inksandbindings.com
orders@inksandbindings.com

As Christians, we believe all manner of things. We believe God to be according to our understanding. We have that right, the trouble begins when we are convinced, we have obtained the proper understanding and run with it.

2 Timothy 3:16
All scripture is given by inspiration of God, and is profitable for doctrine, for reproof, for correction, for instruction in righteousness:

We expose ourselves to perpetuate lies, validate lies and yield our power over to the enemy of our salvation becoming the Devil's advocate. In adding to your faith or belief we become the enemy of God and subject to the wrath of God.

1 Corinthians 14:10
There are, it may be, so many kinds of voices in the world, and none of them is without signification.

There is a purpose, a direction, and an underlining agenda to everything that is preached, sung, and portrayed. The elevated belief causes misguided conclusions, making false accusations about God, trying to justify themselves or their position in the body. I am here to tell you, repent.

2 Thessalonians 2:11-12
And for this cause God shall send them strong delusion, that they should believe a lie: That they all might be damned who believed not the truth, but had pleasure in unrighteousness.

You will affirm the scripture or accuse God by your interpretation inspired by the Devil. When you conclude the Devils interpretation, you affirm, lend creditability to his lies.

2 Timothy 2:15
Study to shew thyself approved unto God, a workman that needeth not to be ashamed, rightly dividing the word of truth.

That is why as Christians we must study, not read, reading will not direct you to rightly divide or think about the direction the scriptures are leading you. Your lack of knowledge and understanding connects you with the Devil and you carry out his agenda perpetuating lies accusing God and the writers of the scriptures. Think, the bible is not compiled with just good stories, it is directing the reader toward questioning God.

James 1:5
If any of you lack wisdom, let him ask of God, that giveth
to all men liberally, and upbraideth not; and it shall be
given him.

Think, the bible in its understanding is not disjointed, it is related to every other scripture and must line up. The scriptures expose liars and false teachers and those who don't know the truth. That's why *study* is very important. Think, the bible sometimes will reveal a thought process by what is written, or not written. It will relate a statement to another passage for you to get a clearer understanding. The *Voice of the Sword* series of books give the reader a spiritual understanding of what is written.

Today's starting point is Genesis 1:1. *Think and follow along.*

Genesis 1:1
In the beginning God created the heaven and the earth.

Genesis 1:1 makes a very important statement, In the beginning God. What the scripture don't say is that God was by himself. Other scriptures describe God as being an eternal being. God being from everlasting to everlasting. You can assume that he was by himself, you would be incorrect. God made the angels to worship him. God is God all by himself, but was he by himself?

Hebrews 1:7
And of the angels he saith, Who maketh his angels spirits, and
his ministers a flame of fire.

Looking further in the scriptures, when God destroyed Sodom and Gomorrah. God was not by himself he came with two angels. Study would them to be Michael and Gabriel. Two angels accompanied Melchizedek when visiting Abraham. The Arc of the covenant, was fashioned with two angels covering the mercy seat with their wings. Think all this time of angels' existence with God, God would never communicate with them. Highly unlikely. Getting back to Moses's explanation of the beginning, because he said it does not mean it occurred. He is explaining the beginning that did not occur until God said let there be light.

Genesis 1:2
And the earth was without form, and void; and darkness was upon the face of the deep. And the Spirit of God moved upon the face of the waters.

The earth was without form, and void; and darkness was upon the face of the deep. And the spirit of God moved upon the face of the waters. Think before the earth was formed, there was darkness and something referring to deep and waters. The spirit of God, as Moses said moved upon the face of the waters. Here is understanding, there was darkness and deep waters that the spirit of God moved upon before the heaven and earth were created. Think If you are not seeing the picture, you are lacking the understanding.

Revelation 17:15 states, "The waters which thou sawest where the whore sitteth, are peoples, multitudes, and nations, and tongues." These people that the spirit of God moved in darkness are the Gentiles. Bible readers don't have a problem with Jesus having a pure bloodline from Adam to Christ, the problem they have is finding the Gentiles.

1 Peter 2:9-10
But ye are a chosen generation, a royal priesthood, an holy nation, a peculiar people; that ye should shew forth the praises of him who hath called you out of darkness into his marvellous light; Which in time past were not a people, but are now the

people of God: which had not obtained mercy, but now have
obtained mercy.

The peoples, nations and multitudes and tongues were before God said let there be light.

Ephesians 1:4
According as he hath chosen us in him before the foundation
of the world, that we should be holy and without blame before
him in love:

John 10:16
And other sheep I have, which are not of this fold: them also
I must bring, and they shall hear my voice; and there shall be
one fold, and one shepherd.

You must study and think rightly dividing the word of truth line upon line.

Proverbs 4:7
Wisdom is the principal thing; therefore get wisdom: and with
all thy getting get understanding.

Everyone that studies the scriptures are not searching to find the truth; they are searching to bring accusations against God or find fault with inconsistencies they find in the bible. If given enough time all those misunderstandings could be explained.

Genesis 1:26
And God said, Let us make man in our image, after our
likeness: and let them have dominion over the fish of the sea,
and over the fowl of the air, and over the cattle, and over all
the earth, and over every creeping thing that creepeth upon
the earth.

Genesis 1:26 is the scripture that causes division even with some believers. Examine the scriptures for what it says. God said *let us*. Stupidity says that he was talking to himself, also speaking to the three parts of him: father, son and spirit. Simply stated his angels that was with him. Who is like him?

Hebrews 1:7
And of the angels he saith, Who maketh his angels spirits, and his ministers a flame of fire.

What of what he made is after his likeness? Angels, as long as God lives, angels will live. As long as God lives man will live. Think and don't miss the point, male and female he blessed them. The Jew, a line of people and blessed.

2 Peter 3:8
But, beloved, be not ignorant of this one thing, that one day is with the Lord as a thousand years, and a thousand years as one day.

How are you thinking of that day? Is it a thousand-year day? Or our 24-hour day? What measuring tool are you using? Scientists carbon date fossils millions of years, but what measuring tool are they using?

Romans 3:4
God forbid: yea, let God be true, but every man a liar; as it is written, That thou mightest be justified in thy sayings, and mightest overcome when thou art judged.

What is your understanding? Hopefully I won't lose you. The bible speaks about you being a witness.

Isaiah 43:10-12
Ye are my witnesses, saith the Lord, and my servant whom I have chosen: that ye may know and believe me, and understand that I am he: before me there was no God formed, neither shall there be after me.

I, even I, am the Lord; and beside me there is no saviour. I have declared, and have saved, and I have shewed, when

*there was no strange god among you: therefore ye are my
witnesses, saith the Lord, that I am God.*

A witness is someone who was there, to see the things taking place.

John 14:26
*But the Comforter, which is the Holy Ghost, whom the Father
will send in my name, he shall teach you all things, and bring all
things to your remembrance, whatsoever I have said unto you.*

The keyword in Jesus's speaking was remembrance, which implies that you heard the statement before. God's word places you in the beginning.

Acts 2:17
*And it shall come to pass in the last days, saith God, I will
pour out of my Spirit upon all flesh: and your sons and your
daughters shall prophesy, and your young men shall see visions,
and your old men shall dream dreams:*

Acts 2:17 causes you to remember, gives you dreams and visions, déjà vu. You witness a place that you never been to in your body, everything is exactly the same. God is opening up your spiritual awareness and understanding, teaching about the part of you that you don't understand. Your part is to diligently seek him.

Hebrews 11:6
*But without faith it is impossible to please him: for he that
cometh to God must believe that he is, and that he is a
rewarder of them that diligently seek him.*

Spiritual understanding is mandatory.

Genesis 2:21-26
*And the Lord God caused a deep sleep to fall upon Adam, and
he slept: and he took one of his ribs, and closed up the flesh
instead thereof;*

*And the rib, which the Lord God had taken from man, made
he a woman, and brought her unto the man.*

*And Adam said, This is now bone of my bones, and flesh of
my flesh: she shall be called Woman, because she was taken
out of Man.*

*Therefore shall a man leave his father and his mother, and
shall cleave unto his wife: and they shall be one flesh.*

*And they were both naked, the man and his wife, and were
not ashamed.*

Man is made in the image of God, a spiritual being, therefore
the man Adam in that form could not till the soil and remember
God created a body for Adam to live in or till the ground. This
communication, fellowship written in the scriptures implies that
the communication he had with God, God had faith confidence of
Adam naming all the animals shows his preexistence. Remember
Adam was also blessed. Studying the scriptures you will find that
Adam had a knowledge that he had been with Jesus, Adam was
asleep; it was documented that the woman was his wife, came from
his bones, his help meet.

Genesis 2:21-26, where did the knowledge of man leaving
father and mother come from? Presenting clear evidence that he
existed before to know these things. Was Genesis 1:26 before the
foundation of the world? Or after? Study will show clearly after.
We have the scriptural evidence of existing before formed in a body.
Ephesians 1:4-6 *Gentiles*, Genesis 1:2, 1 Peter 2:9, Continuing in
Genesis 3, *Think and study* carefully. We know that the serpent is
first mentioned, but his answers clue you in that he existed before
this time.

Revelation 20:2
*And he laid hold on the dragon, that old serpent, which is the
Devil, and Satan, and bound him a thousand years,*

Satan study reveals that he at that time a fallen angel, cast into outer darkness. Is this the same darkness where the gentiles were? Chronological history is vague but makes the declaration that he was a beast. If an angel, angels are spirits that cannot be destroyed, their punishment has to be eternal, everlasting. Scriptures reveal that the Lord God made. Think if there were no opposition in your life would you really get serious with God; he could not do it because he is a loving God and totally against his nature. Satan arrived after there was light, he was interpreting to the woman, how he divided the scriptures, implying prior communication with the Lord. The serpent used Eve's lack of knowledge of the scriptures to believe him instead of God.

Genesis 3:6
And when the woman saw that the tree was good for food,
and that it was pleasant to the eyes, and a tree to be desired to
make one wise, she took of the fruit thereof, and did eat, and
gave also unto her husband with her; and he did eat.

Study the answer Eve gives to the serpent, using the carnal mind to convince her to eat the fruit. The lust of the eye, the pride of life, and the lust of the flesh.

Romans 8:7
Because the carnal mind is enmity against God: for it is not
subject to the law of God, neither indeed can be.

After the fall, Adam accused the woman and the woman accused the serpent. Judgement being given, starting at the serpent, God cursed him and told him what he was going to eat all the days of his life, the byproduct of man. It was also told that he would go on his belly all the days of his life. Who is this, *Lord God?* Only Jesus. Jesus throughout his ministry knowing the thoughts of the people.

Hebrews 13:8
Jesus Christ the same yesterday, and to day, and for ever.

Luke 6:8
But he knew their thoughts, and said to the man which had the withered hand, Rise up, and stand forth in the midst. And he arose and stood forth.

1 John 3:20
For if our heart condemn us, God is greater than our heart, and knoweth all things.

John 5:46
For had ye believed Moses, ye would have believed me; for he wrote of me.

Psalms 100:3
Know ye that the Lord he is God: it is he that hath made us, and not we ourselves; we are his people, and the sheep of his pasture.

Man in his limited knowledge, believe that he can intellectually know and please God using the carnal mind conjure up explanations of scriptures that they don't understand like snakes, trees, and shallow spiritual meanings. The punishment for the serpent was not final, only temporary reserved for the eternal judgment. Jesus being the Lord God spoke in terms of the serpent's seed and the woman's seed that refers to children. He must have known he would have children.

1 John 3:10
In this the children of God are manifest, and the children of the devil: whosoever doeth not righteousness is not of God, neither he that loveth not his brother.

1 John 3:12
Not as Cain, who was of that wicked one, and slew his brother. And wherefore slew he him? Because his own works were evil, and his brother's righteous.

Jesus made the statement that Moses wrote of him. Understanding says that Moses wrote the first five books of the Old Testament where Jesus was not known as Jesus, he was known as the Lord God. 1,513 years from Moses to Jesus Christ.

John 5:46
For had ye believed Moses, ye would have believed me; for he wrote of me.

Think the punishment for Eve was pain in her conception, sorrow, and bring forth children. God is directing us to the understanding, Eve is now ashamed, naked and with child. We established earlier that she was the wife of Adam, now Jesus is giving her back to Adam.

Genesis 3:16
Unto the woman he said, I will greatly multiply thy sorrow and thy conception; in sorrow thou shalt bring forth children; and thy desire shall be to thy husband, and he shall rule over thee.

Without understanding conclusions are being made to explain this fellowship between the serpent and the woman. With their carnal mind they invent a story to explain the circumstances, it doesn't line up. In their explanation they become the devil's advocate accusing Adam of being the father of Cain.

1 John 3:12
Not as Cain, who was of that wicked one, and slew his brother. And wherefore slew he him? Because his own works were evil, and his brother's righteous.

Is Adam the wicked one? With your accusations that would make God wicked, guilty by association. I would re-think that interpretation. Think Before Adam knew his wife, God said she would have pain in her conception, she would bring forth children. She was the mother, who was the father? Who is she trying to convince? I got a man from the Lord. After Adam knew his wife, she brought forth children, males. We know that if Adam produces children the child would have Adam's attributes and God's attributes. Cain had neither, only Abel. God respect for Abel and his sacrifice, God had no respect for his sacrifice or him.

Acts 10:34
Unto the woman he said, I will greatly multiply thy sorrow and thy conception; in sorrow thou shalt bring forth children; and thy desire shall be to thy husband, and he shall rule over thee.

Genesis 4:12
When thou tillest the ground, it shall not henceforth yield unto thee her strength; a fugitive and a vagabond shalt thou be in the earth.

Where did Cain come from? How was he produced? Did God take him from his creation that was blessed? Where did his spirit come from? Think If Adam had a son, he would be a Jew, blessed and have the spirit of God in him to do good. God challenged Cain, "if you do well, I'll accept you." Answering those questions, the serpent by carnal knowledge with Eve, produced his seed, took of the people before the foundation of the world, a gentile produced Cain counterfeiting God's man Adam. You now have enmity, variance and hatred between the two. Notice that the people before the foundation were not blessed which they can be presented and available to be cursed. The serpent's attribute was a beast, if the serpent had a seed he would carry his spirit, his attributes and his nature.

Think…

Genesis 4:11
And now art thou cursed from the earth, which hath opened her mouth to receive thy brother's blood from thy hand;

According to Moses, God cursed Cain just like he cursed his father. A mark was placed on Cain to distinguish him from other people.

Ecclesiastes 3:18-21
I said in mine heart concerning the estate of the sons of men,
that God might manifest them, and that they might see that
they themselves are beasts.

For that which befalleth the sons of men befalleth beasts;
even one thing befalleth them: as the one dieth, so dieth the
other; yea, they have all one breath; so that a man hath no
preeminence above a beast: for all is vanity.

All go unto one place; all are of the dust, and all turn to
dust again.

Who knoweth the spirit of man that goeth upward, and the
spirit of the beast that goeth downward to the earth?

Genesis 6:4
There were giants in the earth in those days; and also after
that, when the sons of God came in unto the daughters of men,
and they bare children to them, the same became mighty men
which were of old, men of renown.

The mixing of the Jew and the gentile is what angered God. These people went out from the presence of God and began to fruitful and multiply on the face of the earth, daughters of men, gentiles God haters, murderers, liars, trying to get back in God's good graces. Now Cain's family, the sons of men, gentiles, God haters, and the like. Continuing to follow the sons of men you will find that they are trying to find another way to heaven, to be acceptable to God by building the tower and God confounded the languages to stop the build.

Genesis 4:25-26
And Adam knew his wife again; and she bare a son, and
called his name Seth: For God, said she, hath appointed me
another seed instead of Abel, whom Cain slew.

And to Seth, to him also there was born a son; and he called his
name Enos: then began men to call upon the name of the Lord.

Of all the people in Cains generation only Seth and his people began to call upon the name of the Lord. *Think, Study,* follow the bloodlines, follow the cursed people, follow the direction the spiritual understanding is leading you. Study will un-lock all the questions you have or had, it will become clearer and clearer of the bible happenings. Let's skip forward a little, although you may not hear the scriptures divided in this manner, study it for yourself.

Luke 8:26-34
And they arrived at the country of the Gadarenes, which is over against Galilee.

And when he went forth to land, there met him out of the city a certain man, which had devils long time, and ware no clothes, neither abode in any house, but in the tombs.

When he saw Jesus, he cried out, and fell down before him, and with a loud voice said, What have I to do with thee, Jesus, thou Son of God most high? I beseech thee, torment me not.

(For he had commanded the unclean spirit to come out of the man. For oftentimes it had caught him: and he was kept bound with chains and in fetters; and he brake the bands, and was driven of the devil into the wilderness.)

And Jesus asked him, saying, What is thy name? And he said, Legion: because many devils were entered into him.

And they besought him that he would not command them to go out into the deep.

And there was there an herd of many swine feeding on the mountain: and they besought him that he would suffer them to enter into them. And he suffered them.

Then went the devils out of the man, and entered into the swine: and the herd ran violently down a steep place into the lake, and were choked.

When they that fed them saw what was done, they fled, and went and told it in the city and in the country.

Is that all? *Think After careful study* of the scriptures this should be clear. What is important about the event is, some say 2 thousand, some say it could be up to five thousand demons cast into the swine. That is not the important part, it is that the demons embodied the swine and the swine was drowned, you can't destroy a spirit by drowning. Those spirits are free from the body it inhabited and now are loosed among us trying to find a home.

2 Thessalonians 2:1–13

Now we beseech you, brethren, by the coming of our Lord Jesus Christ, and by our gathering together unto him,

That ye be not soon shaken in mind, or be troubled, neither by spirit, nor by word, nor by letter as from us, as that the day of Christ is at hand.

Let no man deceive you by any means: for that day shall not come, except there come a falling away first, and that man of sin be revealed, the son of perdition;

Who opposeth and exalteth himself above all that is called God, or that is worshipped; so that he as God sitteth in the temple of God, shewing himself that he is God.

Remember ye not, that, when I was yet with you, I told you these things?

And now ye know what withholdeth that he might be revealed in his time.

For the mystery of iniquity doth already work: only he who now letteth will let, until he be taken out of the way.

And then shall that Wicked be revealed, whom the Lord shall consume with the spirit of his mouth, and shall destroy with the brightness of his coming:

Even him, whose coming is after the working of Satan with all power and signs and lying wonders,

And with all deceivableness of unrighteousness in them that perish; because they received not the love of the truth, that they might be saved.

And for this cause God shall send them strong delusion, that they should believe a lie:

That they all might be damned who believed not the truth, but had pleasure in unrighteousness.

But we are bound to give thanks alway to God for you, brethren beloved of the Lord, because God hath from the beginning chosen you to salvation through sanctification of the Spirit and belief of the truth:

We are in the last days where people can see the signs of the time, looking for God. Looking for someone to tell them the truth, to help them on their journey toward spiritual enlightenment and to find God. This a time where we are experiencing not only a drought and a famine at the same time.

Amos 8:11-12

Behold, the days come, saith the Lord God, that I will send a famine in the land, not a famine of bread, nor a thirst for water, but of hearing the words of the Lord:

And they shall wander from sea to sea, and from the north even to the east, they shall run to and fro to seek the word of the Lord, and shall not find it.

Lots of opposition you face when you see Jesus is the way, you try to straighten out your life, some false preacher or false teacher confuses you on the way to get to God. You are presented with those spirits trying to convince you to accuse the bible of being false, God being a mean person and convince you to blame God for the violence, turmoil and chaos that the world is experiencing.

Matthew 12:43–45

When the unclean spirit is gone out of a man, he walketh through dry places, seeking rest, and findeth none.

Then he saith, I will return into my house from whence I came out; and when he is come, he findeth it empty, swept, and garnished.

Then goeth he, and taketh with himself seven other spirits more wicked than himself, and they enter in and dwell there: and the last state of that man is worse than the first. Even so shall it be also unto this wicked generation.

Matthew 24:4–29

And Jesus answered and said unto them, Take heed that no man deceive you.

For many shall come in my name, saying, I am Christ; and shall deceive many.

And ye shall hear of wars and rumours of wars: see that ye be not troubled: for all these things must come to pass, but the end is not yet.

For nation shall rise against nation, and kingdom against kingdom: and there shall be famines, and pestilences, and earthquakes, in divers places.

All these are the beginning of sorrows.

Then shall they deliver you up to be afflicted, and shall kill you: and ye shall be hated of all nations for my name's sake.

And then shall many be offended, and shall betray one another, and shall hate one another.

And many false prophets shall rise, and shall deceive many.

And because iniquity shall abound, the love of many shall wax cold.

But he that shall endure unto the end, the same shall be saved.

And this gospel of the kingdom shall be preached in all the world for a witness unto all nations; and then shall the end come.

When ye therefore shall see the abomination of desolation, spoken of by Daniel the prophet, stand in the holy place, (whoso readeth, let him understand:)

Then let them which be in Judaea flee into the mountains:

Let him which is on the housetop not come down to take any thing out of his house:

Neither let him which is in the field return back to take his clothes.

And woe unto them that are with child, and to them that give suck in those days!

But pray ye that your flight be not in the winter, neither on the sabbath day:

For then shall be great tribulation, such as was not since the beginning of the world to this time, no, nor ever shall be.

And except those days should be shortened, there should no flesh be saved: but for the elect's sake those days shall be shortened.

Then if any man shall say unto you, Lo, here is Christ, or there; believe it not.

For there shall arise false Christs, and false prophets, and shall shew great signs and wonders; insomuch that, if it were possible, they shall deceive the very elect.

Behold, I have told you before.

Wherefore if they shall say unto you, Behold, he is in the desert; go not forth: behold, he is in the secret chambers; believe it not.

For as the lightning cometh out of the east, and shineth even unto the west; so shall also the coming of the Son of man be.

For wheresoever the carcase is, there will the eagles be gathered together.

Immediately after the tribulation of those days shall the sun be darkened, and the moon shall not give her light, and the stars shall fall from heaven, and the powers of the heavens shall be shaken:

You start out trying to clean up your life then you stop opening yourself to those spirits. You are made to believe that the devil was the baddest in the land, when he takes with him 7 other spirits wicked than himself. You are outnumbered and at a disadvantage.

Romans 10:14-15
How then shall they call on him in whom they have not believed? and how shall they believe in him of whom they have not heard? and how shall they hear without a preacher?

And how shall they preach, except they be sent? as it is written, How beautiful are the feet of them that preach the gospel of peace, and bring glad tidings of good things!

Consider what you believe, how you believe, and most important the actions that you add to your belief. Free yourself from the tricks of the devil and don't become his accuser and advocate. Your power is to be used for good.

Matthew 6:10
Thy kingdom come, Thy will be done in earth, as it is in heaven.

Referred to as the Lord's prayer, many accuse the Lord of taking ownership of it. Study reveals that it was not the Lord's prayer but the prayer taught to the disciples on how to pray, often misquoted by saying, "on" earth instead of "in" earth as the scripture says, God's will will never be done on earth, only in earth, in your body surrendering your will over to the lord. Another accusation stated about God's person Abraham, believed to have lied to obtain the blessing.

Genesis 20:12
And yet indeed she is my sister; she is the daughter of my father,
but not the daughter of my mother; and she became my wife.

Study will show that indeed Sarah was his sister and Abraham did not lie to Abimelech to obtain the blessing. Accusations of Abraham lying is continuing thru his son Isaac saying that he lied about Rebecca being his sister. Every mystery in the scriptures is not revealed to me but what I will say is that you need to be careful what you are concluding. We know that Rebecca was close in relationship to Abraham and Isaac. You conclude he was lying, by your mouth and your statement you condemn yourself.

1 Timothy 5:1-2
And yet indeed she is my sister; she is the daughter of my father,
but not the daughter of my mother; and she became my wife.

If you use the scriptures in 1 Timothy 5:1-2 calling your wife sister so and so, women with age, mothers you are lying. I do not know everything but what I will not do is accuse someone of lying.

John 3:11
Verily, verily, I say unto thee, We speak that we do know, and
testify that we have seen; and ye receive not our witness.

Maybe, God was changing a situation like naming John the Baptist, John then allowing Jesus to have a name not of his relatives and no longer using titles described in the Old Testament. Did you get that conclusion from God? Or are you jumping to conclusions accusing and becoming the Devil's advocate?

Leviticus 18:7-8
The nakedness of thy father, or the nakedness of thy mother,
shalt thou not uncover: she is thy mother; thou shalt not
uncover her nakedness.

The nakedness of thy father's wife shalt thou not uncover: it is thy father's nakedness.

Reading the scriptures and not studying them you won't get a clear understanding of what the writer is explaining. Noah was drunk in his tent, that is established. Ham is the father, that is established. Canaan got off the arc. Ask yourself who was Canaan's mother? What was it about Noah's tent that got Ham's attention? Everybody has their own tent for them and their wives. Ham sinned, why was the baby cursed? The third person in the beginning cursed, God blessed them as they exited the arc. Noah could not curse him because he was blessed. He cursed Cannan. Follow the people or bloodline of him, the attributes and the nature of them.

Genesis 10:15-19
And Canaan begat Sidon his first born, and Heth,
And the Jebusite, and the Amorite, and the Girgasite,
And the Hivite, and the Arkite, and the Sinite,

And the Arvadite, and the Zemarite, and the Hamathite: and afterward were the families of the Canaanites spread abroad.

And the border of the Canaanites was from Sidon, as thou comest to Gerar, unto Gaza; as thou goest, unto Sodom, and Gomorrah, and Admah, and Zeboim, even unto Lasha.

The series of events when Ham exited his father's tent, putting a cloth on their shoulders, walking backward in the tent only makes sense if it was out of respect for their mother in the father's tent.

Revelation 11:1-2
And there was given me a reed like unto a rod: and the angel stood, saying, Rise, and measure the temple of God, and the altar, and them that worship therein.

But the court which is without the temple leave out, and measure it not; for it is given unto the Gentiles: and the holy city shall they tread under foot forty and two months.

42 months is equal to 3 and a half years. Is it a coincidence that God will save of the 12 tribes of Israel 144 thousand and the outer courts number were left out.

2 Samuel 24:11-13

For when David was up in the morning, the word of the Lord came unto the prophet Gad, David's seer, saying,

Go and say unto David, Thus saith the Lord, I offer thee three things; choose thee one of them, that I may do it unto thee.

So Gad came to David, and told him, and said unto him, Shall seven years of famine come unto thee in thy land? or wilt thou flee three months before thine enemies, while they pursue thee? or that there be three days' pestilence in thy land? now advise, and see what answer I shall return to him that sent me.

Hebrews 11:1-40

Now faith is the substance of things hoped for, the evidence of things not seen.

For by it the elders obtained a good report.

Through faith we understand that the worlds were framed by the word of God, so that things which are seen were not made of things which do appear.

By faith Abel offered unto God a more excellent sacrifice than Cain, by which he obtained witness that he was righteous, God testifying of his gifts: and by it he being dead yet speaketh.

By faith Enoch was translated that he should not see death; and was not found, because God had translated him: for before his translation he had this testimony, that he pleased God.

But without faith it is impossible to please him: for he that cometh to God must believe that he is, and that he is a rewarder of them that diligently seek him.

By faith Noah, being warned of God of things not seen as yet, moved with fear, prepared an ark to the saving of his house; by the which he condemned the world, and became heir of the righteousness which is by faith.

By faith Abraham, when he was called to go out into a place which he should after receive for an inheritance, obeyed; and he went out, not knowing whither he went.

By faith he sojourned in the land of promise, as in a strange country, dwelling in tabernacles with Isaac and Jacob, the heirs with him of the same promise:

For he looked for a city which hath foundations, whose builder and maker is God.

Through faith also Sara herself received strength to conceive seed, and was delivered of a child when she was past age, because she judged him faithful who had promised.

Therefore sprang there even of one, and him as good as dead, so many as the stars of the sky in multitude, and as the sand which is by the sea shore innumerable.

These all died in faith, not having received the promises, but having seen them afar off, and were persuaded of them, and embraced them, and confessed that they were strangers and pilgrims on the earth.

For they that say such things declare plainly that they seek a country.

And truly, if they had been mindful of that country from whence they came out, they might have had opportunity to have returned.

But now they desire a better country, that is, an heavenly: wherefore God is not ashamed to be called their God: for he hath prepared for them a city.

By faith Abraham, when he was tried, offered up Isaac: and he that had received the promises offered up his only begotten son,

Of whom it was said, That in Isaac shall thy seed be called:

Accounting that God was able to raise him up, even from the dead; from whence also he received him in a figure.

By faith Isaac blessed Jacob and Esau concerning things to come.

By faith Jacob, when he was a dying, blessed both the sons of Joseph; and worshipped, leaning upon the top of his staff.

By faith Joseph, when he died, made mention of the departing of the children of Israel; and gave commandment concerning his bones.

By faith Moses, when he was born, was hid three months of his parents, because they saw he was a proper child; and they were not afraid of the king's commandment.

By faith Moses, when he was come to years, refused to be called the son of Pharaoh's daughter;

Choosing rather to suffer affliction with the people of God, than to enjoy the pleasures of sin for a season;

Esteeming the reproach of Christ greater riches than the treasures in Egypt: for he had respect unto the recompence of the reward.

By faith he forsook Egypt, not fearing the wrath of the king: for he endured, as seeing him who is invisible.

Through faith he kept the passover, and the sprinkling of blood, lest he that destroyed the firstborn should touch them.

By faith they passed through the Red sea as by dry land: which the Egyptians assaying to do were drowned.

By faith the walls of Jericho fell down, after they were compassed about seven days.

By faith the harlot Rahab perished not with them that believed not, when she had received the spies with peace.

And what shall I more say? for the time would fail me to tell of Gedeon, and of Barak, and of Samson, and of Jephthae; of David also, and Samuel, and of the prophets:

Who through faith subdued kingdoms, wrought righteousness, obtained promises, stopped the mouths of lions.

Quenched the violence of fire, escaped the edge of the sword, out of weakness were made strong, waxed valiant in fight, turned to flight the armies of the aliens.

Women received their dead raised to life again: and others were tortured, not accepting deliverance; that they might obtain a better resurrection:

And others had trial of cruel mockings and scourgings, yea, moreover of bonds and imprisonment:

They were stoned, they were sawn asunder, were tempted, were slain with the sword: they wandered about in sheepskins and goatskins; being destitute, afflicted, tormented;

(Of whom the world was not worthy:) they wandered in deserts, and in mountains, and in dens and caves of the earth.

And these all, having obtained a good report through faith, received not the promise:

God having provided some better thing for us, that they without us should not be made perfect.

He that is last shall be first and he that is first shall be last. The children of faith kept in the third heaven waiting for the latter saints to be perfected.

Revelation 11:3

And I will give power unto my two witnesses, and they shall prophesy a thousand two hundred and threescore days, clothed in sackcloth.

Also, almost 3 and a half years. If God would choose to bind the serpent that amount of time, no one could discern the day or the hour with the 7 spirits more wicked than himself unleashed in the world. Think It's later than you think.

Daniel 3:10-30

Thou, O king, hast made a decree, that every man that shall hear the sound of the cornet, flute, harp, sackbut, psaltery, and dulcimer, and all kinds of musick, shall fall down and worship the golden image:

And whoso falleth not down and worshippeth, that he should be cast into the midst of a burning fiery furnace.

There are certain Jews whom thou hast set over the affairs of the province of Babylon, Shadrach, Meshach, and Abednego; these men, O king, have not regarded thee: they serve not thy gods, nor worship the golden image which thou hast set up.

Then Nebuchadnezzar in his rage and fury commanded to bring Shadrach, Meshach, and Abednego. Then they brought these men before the king.

Nebuchadnezzar spake and said unto them, Is it true, O Shadrach, Meshach, and Abednego, do not ye serve my gods, nor worship the golden image which I have set up?

Now if ye be ready that at what time ye hear the sound of the cornet, flute, harp, sackbut, psaltery, and dulcimer, and all kinds of musick, ye fall down and worship the image which I have made; well: but if ye worship not, ye shall be cast the same hour into the midst of a burning fiery furnace; and who is that God that shall deliver you out of my hands?

Shadrach, Meshach, and Abednego, answered and said to the king, O Nebuchadnezzar, we are not careful to answer thee in this matter.

If it be so, our God whom we serve is able to deliver us from the burning fiery furnace, and he will deliver us out of thine hand, O king.

But if not, be it known unto thee, O king, that we will not serve thy gods, nor worship the golden image which thou hast set up.

Then was Nebuchadnezzar full of fury, and the form of his visage was changed against Shadrach, Meshach, and Abednego: therefore he spake, and commanded that they should heat the furnace one seven times more than it was wont to be heated.

And he commanded the most mighty men that were in his army to bind Shadrach, Meshach, and Abednego, and to cast them into the burning fiery furnace.

Then these men were bound in their coats, their hosen, and their hats, and their other garments, and were cast into the midst of the burning fiery furnace.

Therefore because the king's commandment was urgent, and the furnace exceeding hot, the flames of the fire slew those men that took up Shadrach, Meshach, and Abednego.

And these three men, Shadrach, Meshach, and Abednego, fell down bound into the midst of the burning fiery furnace.

Then Nebuchadnezzar the king was astonished, and rose up in haste, and spake, and said unto his counsellors, Did not we cast three men bound into the midst of the fire? They answered and said unto the king, True, O king.

He answered and said, Lo, I see four men loose, walking in the midst of the fire, and they have no hurt; and the form of the fourth is like the Son of God.

Then Nebuchadnezzar came near to the mouth of the burning fiery furnace, and spake, and said, Shadrach, Meshach, and Abednego, ye servants of the most high God, come forth, and come hither. Then Shadrach, Meshach, and Abednego, came forth of the midst of the fire.

And the princes, governors, and captains, and the king's counsellors, being gathered together, saw these men, upon whose bodies the fire had no power, nor was an hair of their head singed, neither were their coats changed, nor the smell of fire had passed on them.

Then Nebuchadnezzar spake, and said, Blessed be the God of Shadrach, Meshach, and Abednego, who hath sent his angel, and delivered his servants that trusted in him, and have changed the king's word, and yielded their bodies, that they might not serve nor worship any god, except their own God.

Therefore I make a decree, That every people, nation, and language, which speak any thing amiss against the God of Shadrach, Meshach, and Abednego, shall be cut in pieces, and their houses shall be made a dunghill: because there is no other God that can deliver after this sort.

Then the king promoted Shadrach, Meshach, and Abednego, in the province of Babylon.

People not obtaining spiritual understanding of the scriptures, stuck on stupid, make accusations about God, they conclude that God was the fourth man in the fire. What did he do? That is such a weak display of God's power. Where was Daniel? Did he bow to the image?

Hebrews 12:29
For our God is a consuming fire.

Rightly divide the word. What did the fire do? Heated 7 times hotter, consumed the strong men, removed the bands that had them bound, allowed them to walk in the midst and not die smell of smoke and all.

Psalms 24:8
Who is this King of glory? The Lord strong and mighty,
the Lord mighty in battle.

God is all that and much more, the fire. Search the scriptures of how many times God appeared representing fire. The flaming sword, to keep the way of the tree of life, contest at Mt. Carmel, answering by fire.

Hosea 4:6
My people are destroyed for lack of knowledge: because thou
hast rejected knowledge, I will also reject thee, that thou shalt
be no priest to me: seeing thou hast forgotten the law of thy
God, I will also forget thy children.

Because of a lack of knowledge, re-think the conclusions you make, the interpretations you believe, you could be condemning yourself by lending your power, creditability and accusations to things not according to the scriptures. *Think, Study* and ask God.

1 John 4:1-4
Beloved, believe not every spirit, but try the spirits whether
they are of God: because many false prophets are gone out into
the world.

Hereby know ye the Spirit of God: Every spirit that confesseth
that Jesus Christ is come in the flesh is of God:

And every spirit that confesseth not that Jesus Christ is come
in the flesh is not of God: and this is that spirit of antichrist,

whereof ye have heard that it should come; and even now already is it in the world.

Ye are of God, little children, and have overcome them: because greater is he that is in you, than he that is in the world.

Ephesians 6:10-13

Finally, my brethren, be strong in the Lord, and in the power of his might.

Put on the whole armour of God, that ye may be able to stand against the wiles of the devil.

For we wrestle not against flesh and blood, but against principalities, against powers, against the rulers of the darkness of this world, against spiritual wickedness in high places.

Wherefore take unto you the whole armour of God, that ye may be able to withstand in the evil day, and having done all, to stand.

Acts 10:8-17

And when he had declared all these things unto them, he sent them to Joppa.

On the morrow, as they went on their journey, and drew nigh unto the city, Peter went up upon the housetop to pray about the sixth hour:

And he became very hungry, and would have eaten: but while they made ready, he fell into a trance,

And saw heaven opened, and a certain vessel descending upon him, as it had been a great sheet knit at the four corners, and let down to the earth:

Wherein were all manner of fourfooted beasts of the earth, and wild beasts, and creeping things, and fowls of the air.

And there came a voice to him, Rise, Peter; kill, and eat.

But Peter said, Not so, Lord; for I have never eaten any thing that is common or unclean.

And the voice spake unto him again the second time, What God hath cleansed, that call not thou common.

This was done thrice: and the vessel was received up again into heaven.

Now while Peter doubted in himself what this vision which he had seen should mean, behold, the men which were sent from Cornelius had made enquiry for Simon's house, and stood before the gate,

John 18:10-11
Then Simon Peter having a sword drew it, and smote the high priest's servant, and cut off his right ear. The servant's name was Malchus.

Then said Jesus unto Peter, Put up thy sword into the sheath: the cup which my Father hath given me, shall I not drink it?

Consider Peter's life, ministry and his interpretation of things. The transfiguration of Jesus, moved by fear made the statement " it is good for us to be here," Acts 10:8-17 Peter cut the ear off and Jesus put it back. John 18:10-11 He cursed and denied, believing that he was doing the right thing putting action to his belief.

Acts 1:15-26
And in those days Peter stood up in the midst of the disciples, and said, (the number of names together were about an hundred and twenty,)

Men and brethren, this scripture must needs have been fulfilled, which the Holy Ghost by the mouth of David spake before concerning Judas, which was guide to them that took Jesus.

For he was numbered with us, and had obtained part of this ministry.

Now this man purchased a field with the reward of iniquity; and falling headlong, he burst asunder in the midst, and all his bowels gushed out.

And it was known unto all the dwellers at Jerusalem; insomuch as that field is called in their proper tongue, Aceldama, that is to say, The field of blood.

For it is written in the book of Psalms, Let his habitation be desolate, and let no man dwell therein: and his bishoprick let another take.

Wherefore of these men which have companied with us all the time that the Lord Jesus went in and out among us,

Beginning from the baptism of John, unto that same day that he was taken up from us, must one be ordained to be a witness with us of his resurrection.

And they appointed two, Joseph called Barsabas, who was surnamed Justus, and Matthias.

And they prayed, and said, Thou, Lord, which knowest the hearts of all men, shew whether of these two thou hast chosen,

That he may take part of this ministry and apostleship, from which Judas by transgression fell, that he might go to his own place.

And they gave forth their lots; and the lot fell upon Matthias; and he was numbered with the eleven apostles.

Although misguided Peter continued until he received understanding rightly dividing the word, the rebuke of Jesus on the roof. All these things were done before he received the Holy Ghost, receiving power and the spirit of God. Christians with their dirty lives, full of all the sins God hates, try to clean their lives and bodies never continue to receiving the power, convince themselves that they are doing the right thing, finding their body clean and swept for the Devil and his seven joining together to re-enter.

Matthew 24:4–31

And Jesus answered and said unto them, Take heed that no man deceive you.

For many shall come in my name, saying, I am Christ; and shall deceive many.

And ye shall hear of wars and rumours of wars: see that ye be not troubled: for all these things must come to pass, but the end is not yet.

For nation shall rise against nation, and kingdom against kingdom: and there shall be famines, and pestilences, and earthquakes, in divers places.

All these are the beginning of sorrows.

Then shall they deliver you up to be afflicted, and shall kill you: and ye shall be hated of all nations for my name's sake.

And then shall many be offended, and shall betray one another, and shall hate one another.

And many false prophets shall rise, and shall deceive many.

And because iniquity shall abound, the love of many shall wax cold.

But he that shall endure unto the end, the same shall be saved.

And this gospel of the kingdom shall be preached in all the world for a witness unto all nations; and then shall the end come.

When ye therefore shall see the abomination of desolation, spoken of by Daniel the prophet, stand in the holy place, (whoso readeth, let him understand:)

Then let them which be in Judaea flee into the mountains:

Let him which is on the housetop not come down to take any thing out of his house:

Neither let him which is in the field return back to take his clothes.

And woe unto them that are with child, and to them that give suck in those days!

But pray ye that your flight be not in the winter, neither on the sabbath day:

For then shall be great tribulation, such as was not since the beginning of the world to this time, no, nor ever shall be.

And except those days should be shortened, there should no flesh be saved: but for the elect's sake those days shall be shortened.

Then if any man shall say unto you, Lo, here is Christ, or there; believe it not.

For there shall arise false Christs, and false prophets, and shall shew great signs and wonders; insomuch that, if it were possible, they shall deceive the very elect.

Behold, I have told you before.

Wherefore if they shall say unto you, Behold, he is in the desert; go not forth: behold, he is in the secret chambers; believe it not.

For as the lightning cometh out of the east, and shineth even unto the west; so shall also the coming of the Son of man be.

For wheresoever the carcase is, there will the eagles be gathered together.

Immediately after the tribulation of those days shall the sun be darkened, and the moon shall not give her light, and the stars

*shall fall from heaven, and the powers of the heavens shall
be shaken:*

*And then shall appear the sign of the Son of man in heaven:
and then shall all the tribes of the earth mourn, and they shall
see the Son of man coming in the clouds of heaven with power
and great glory.*

*And he shall send his angels with a great sound of a trumpet,
and they shall gather together his elect from the four winds,
from one end of heaven to the other.*

God will not make any exceptions for anyone. If you ever come in contact with the spirit of God, feel his presence, it is the spirit that gives you power over whatever ails you. Don't be delusional.

Isaiah 35:8-9
*And an highway shall be there, and a way, and it shall be
called The way of holiness; the unclean shall not pass over it;
but it shall be for those: the wayfaring men, though fools, shall
not err therein.*

*No lion shall be there, nor any ravenous beast shall go up
thereon, it shall not be found there; but the redeemed shall
walk there:*

Do you really have the spirit of God living in you? Or are you playing church?

www.ingramcontent.com/pod-product-compliance
Lightning Source LLC
Chambersburg PA
CBHW061722120626
46550CB00003B/1326